TO THE LION THRONE

TO THE LION THRONE

THE STORY OF THE FOURTEENTH DALAI LAMA

by

Whitney Stewart

Snow Lion Publications
Ithaca, New York

Snow Lion Publications
P.O. Box 6483
Ithaca, NY 14851
USA

Printed in the USA

ISBN 0-937938-75-0

Library of Congress Cataloging-in-Publication Data.
Stewart, Whitney, 1959-
     To the lion throne: the story of the 14th Dalai Lama/ by
Whitney Stewart.
        p.   cm.
        Includes bibliographical references.
        ISBN 0-937938-75-0
        1. Bstan'dzin-rgya-mtsho, Dalai Lama XIV, 1935- --Juvenile
literature. 2. Dalai lamas--Biography--Juvenile literature. I. Title.
BQ7935.B777S74 1990
294.3'923'092--dc20
[B]   90-42712
                                    CIP
                                    AC

Acknowledgments

Many people have given me financial, editorial, and emotional support for the making of this book. I want to thank several family members for their sponsorship and their unending confidence: Mr. and Mrs. H.F. Whitney Jr., A. George Scherer III, Carlin W. Scherer, Richard R. Stewart, Cynthia E. Stewart, and my good friend, Mrs. Eleanor Barzin. I also thank many people who have given their time and have answered many questions: Naomi S. Baron, Tenzin Choedak, Jean Fritz, Kelsang Gonshar, Mr. & Mrs. Ted Groll, Khenpo K. Gyaltsen, Heinrich Harrer, Thubten J. Norbu, Nyima Phentok, Sidney Piburn, Alak J. Rinpoche, Doboom Rinpoche, Lama Samtan, Tenzin Sangpo, Deborah Short, the Soepa Family, Mr. & Mrs. Phuntsok T. Takla, Tenzin N. Taklha, Tenzin Geyche Tethong, Thupten Woser, the Office of Tibet in New York, the Tibetan Information Office, and the monks of Namgyal Monastery. I am grateful to my husband, Hans C. Andersson, for his patience and good advice.

And finally, I thank His Holiness the Dalai Lama who dug into his memory to answer my questions, and who made me laugh throughout the interviews.

                                        WS

I dedicate this book to all of my parents and to Tibetans everywhere.

The Western Gateway to Lhasa, Tibet

MAP OF TIBET AND SURROUNDING AREAS

general area inhabited by Tibetans

political boundary in 1959

◆ Lhasa- capital of Tibet

◆ Kumbum- near birthplace of the Dalai Lama

◆ Dharamsala- present seat of Tibetan government-in-exile

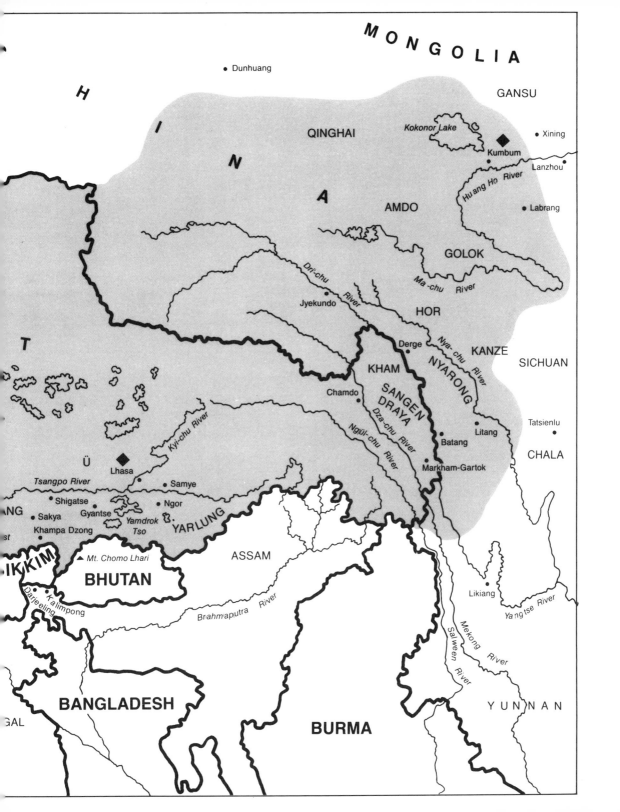

M O N G O L I A

• Dunhuang

GANSU

QINGHAI

Kokonor Lake

◆ Kumbum

• Xining

Hu ang Ho River

Lanzhou

N

A

AMDO

• Labrang

GOLOK

Dri-chu

Ma-chu River

• Jyekundo

River

HOR

I

T

Derge

Nya-chu River

KANZE

SICHUAN

KHAM

SANGEN
DRAYA

NYARONG

• Chamdo

Dza-chu River

• Litang

• Tatsienlu

Kyi-chu River

Ngül-chu River

• Batang

CHALA

Ü

◆

Lhasa

• Samye

Markham-Gartok

Tsangpo River

• Shigatse

• Ngor

ANG

• Sakya

Gyantse

*Yamdrok
Tso*

YARLUNG

Khampa Dzong

st

▲ *Mt. Chomo Lhari*

ASSAM

• Likiang

Yangtse River

IKKIM

BHUTAN

Darjeeling

• Kalimpong

Brahmaputra River

Mekong River

Salween River

GAL

BANGLADESH

BURMA

Y U N N A N

THE DALAI LAMA

FOREWORD

In this book children can read the story of my life,
from my early childhood in a village in eastern Tibet and
my youth in Lhasa, our splendid capital city, to my escape
from Tibet and exile in India. When I was young I used to
hear about other countries and longed to know more about
their people and the way they lived. Although I knew only
Tibetan then, I was able to learn and discover many
interesting things mainly through pictorial books and
magazines. I hope that this book may inspire its readers to
take an interest in the Tibetan people, whose ancient
customs and way of life are presently in danger of
vanishing from the face of the earth.

March 24, 1989

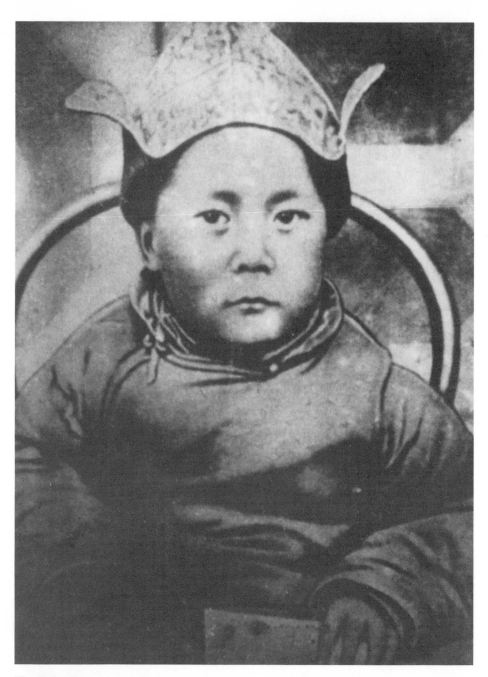

The Dalai Lama at age four

ONE
Riding to Lhasa

IN A LAND CALLED TIBET WHERE THE HIGH-est mountains in the world are still growing taller, where the snow leopard and the yak roam, there was a two-year-old boy named Lhamo Dhondup. He liked to sit on a windowsill and pretend that he was riding to the capital city. His mother, Deyki Tsering, loved him deeply. She smiled at him as she boiled tea for her family, and wondered how such a young boy invented these funny ideas of travelling.

"Ama. I am riding a horse to Lhasa," Lhamo Dhondup told his mother.

She laughed and continued to knead her bread dough. She was a good cook and knew how to make many types of bread and pastries. For breakfast, she served thick brown bread, tea and hard cream. Lhamo Dhondup wiped his bread through the cream and smacked his lips as he ate. He liked to be near his mother who was gentle and patient.

Nobody knew back then that Lhamo would become a great leader.

Avalokiteshvara, the deity who represents perfect compassion. Tibetans believe the
Dalai Lama to be an embodiment of this perfect compassion.

TWO
Under the Crow's Watch

ON THE FIFTH DAY OF THE FIFTH MONTH of the Tibetan Wood Hog Year, Lhamo Dhondup was born into a poor farming family. They lived in Taktser, a village in eastern Tibet. Lhamo was born in a cow shed. As soon as he was born his oldest sister, Tsering Dolma, who was already a teenager, bathed her baby brother and fed him a special herb tea. This was a custom in Taktser. At first one of Lhamo's eyes was half shut, and his sister gently opened it with her fingers. She was the first person to hold the newborn baby, and she became one of his closest friends.

On the day of Lhamo's birth, there were unusual signs that foretold the greatness of the boy, but nobody paid close attention. The weather was dark and thundering, but some people saw a rainbow touching the baby's house. Other neighbors noticed that a pair of noisy crows came to perch on the family's rooftop, as if to watch over the family. The boy's father, Choekyong Tsering, had been very sick for weeks, but on that day he got up feeling perfectly fine. He was grateful for his good health.

"In thanks for my good health, I will make my son a monk," said Choekyong Tsering.

THREE
The Mountain that Pierces the Sky

TO THE SOUTH OF TAKTSER, THERE IS A high mountain that Tibetans call Ami-chiri or The Mountain that Pierces the Sky. People say that this is the home of the protector of the land. On the summit, there is a patch of snow that never melts, and below, deer, bears and monkeys roam the mountain slopes.

Early every morning, Lhamo's mother prepared offerings to Tibetan Buddhist deities. On the family altar she lit butterlamps that burned with a soft glow like candles. Then the parents and children offered prayers. After that, Lhamo's mother and father burned incense in a clay fireplace in their courtyard.

Lhamo's mother took her infant with her when she went to work in the wheat and barley fields. She tied an umbrella to a stake in the ground to cover her sleeping son. When the boy could walk, he followed his mother on her chores. He helped her collect fresh milk and tend their vegetable garden. Inside the house, Lhamo watched his mother cook. She often made his favorite food— tukpa, a noodle soup of meat broth.

Lhamo Dhondup had six brothers and sisters in all. His oldest brother, Thubten Jigme Norbu, was twelve years older. He lived as a monk in the nearby Kumbum Monastery. His oldest sister, Tsering Dolma, was sweet to her brother, and acted like a second mother. Lhamo felt closest to his brother Lobsang Samten, who was two years older. They fought constantly—Lhamo bullied Lobsang who was meek and never bullied back. Still, the brothers played together inseparably while they were young.

Animals were Lhamo Dhondup's great playmates. One day nobody could find the boy for hours until they discovered him in a chicken coop imitating chicken noises.

When animals fought with each other, Lhamo immediately stepped in to rescue the weaker one. Fear never stopped him; he could even pick up a scorpion. The only creatures he disliked were caterpillars. Looking at them, he always felt an eerie tingling sensation inside.

FOUR
Answer in the East

TWO YEARS BEFORE LHAMO WAS BORN, Tibet's great leader died. The leader of Tibet is known as the Dalai Lama, which means "Great Ocean of Wisdom" in the Mongolian language. The Dalai Lama is said to be wise and full of love for all beings. Tibetans believe that when the Dalai Lama or any great teacher dies, his spirit can be found again in a new baby.

This is called reincarnation. Tibetans believe that all living things are reincarnated or born again after they die. However, only a very few great beings can be recognized in their next lives. Reincarnations of great teachers are called incarnate lamas or incarnations.

After the Thirteenth Dalai Lama died in 1933, the Regent took over the government until he could find the reborn leader. Finding the boy was not easy. The Regent had to look for clues. The new Dalai Lama could be anywhere across Tibet, from the mountains to the valleys.

The first clue was strange. When the Thirteenth Dalai Lama died, his body was placed on a throne in the summer palace, Norbulingka, and it was facing south. A few days later, the face was looking east. The Regent knew that he must look for the new leader in the east of Tibet.

Another clue was found on the northeast side of
the tomb of the Thirteenth Dalai Lama. There, a
curious star-shaped fungus appeared. As for the third
clue, people said that unusual clouds floated into the
northeast sky beyond Lhasa. Always the northeast—the
Regent knew that this clue was important.

In 1935, the Regent travelled to a sacred lake called
Lhamoi Latso. Tibetans believe that skilled monks can
see the future in the waters of this lake. The Regent sat
down and meditated on the shore for several days.
Finally, he saw the picture of three Tibetan letters: Ah,
Ka, and Ma. He also saw the vision of a monastery with
a roof of jade and gold, and a dirt house standing behind
an old poplar tree. He wrote down all of these clues and
kept them secret.

The Thirteenth Dalai Lama

FIVE
Lamas in the Kitchen

THE NEXT YEAR, THE REGENT SENT OUT religious and government officials across Tibet on a search for the new Dalai Lama. One important lama, named Kyitsang Rinpoche, went to the northeast, a trip that took months of trudging through snow. Just as soon as the Rinpoche and his attendants reached the area called Amdo, they came upon the Kumbum monastery with its jade and gold roof. They guessed that the letters Ah, Ka and Ma might be connected to this area: Ah for Amdo, Ka for Kumbum Monastery, and Ka and Ma together for the little monastery of Karma Rolpai Dorje which stood on the mountain above the village of Taktser. Then they saw the dirt house behind the tree. It was Lhamo's house.

The officials discussed their plan to find the child. They decided to disguise themselves and not give away the purpose of their visit. Four men went to the dirt house. Kyitsang Rinpoche disguised himself as a servant by putting a sheepskin cloak over his monk robes. This way he could enter the back door into the kitchen where Lhamo Dhondup was playing. As soon as Lhamo saw the man in the sheepskin cloak, he ran over to him and sat in his lap. The disguised man had a strand of holy beads around his neck. The boy grabbed at them and wanted to keep them.

"You may have the beads if you can guess who I am," said the Rinpoche.

Another monk pointed to the disguised Kyitsang Rinpoche and asked Lhamo, "Who is this man?"

"Sera lama," said Lhamo Dhondup.

He knew that Kyitsang Rinpoche came from Sera Monastery in Lhasa. He also recognized the other monks in the room.

The Rinpoche had to hide his excitement. He knew that he had found the right child, but he could not give away the secret too soon. The men had more tests for the boy. When the Rinpoche started to leave, Lhamo ran to him and asked to be taken with the monks. Kyitsang Rinpoche told Lhamo Dhondup to stay at home, and he promised to return.

For many days after this visit, Lhamo ran around asking when the men would come back. Every time his dog barked, Lhamo went to the front gate and looked out for his friends.

"Please make some tea," Lhamo asked his mother.

Tibetans always offer tea to visitors. Lhamo thought that this might bring the men back. Lhamo was excited and spent his time collecting things in the kitchen.

"I'm packing to go to Lhasa," Lhamo told his mother.

Meanwhile, the Rinpoche stayed at the Kumbum monastery with his attendants. He waited for the right moment to return to Lhamo's house. When they finally decided to make their second visit, they set out from Kumbum. Lifting their heads, they heard the hollow tune of the sacred conch shell, and the song of a cuckoo bird. Soon, they passed men on the road who were carrying yogurt, milk and water. The Rinpoche and his men believed these events to be good omens.

This time the Rinpoche did not disguise himself. When Lhamo's mother saw him at her door, she was startled. The Rinpoche, wearing his gold colored robes, told Lhamo's mother that he was looking for an incarnation. He did not, however, tell her that he was looking for the next Dalai Lama.

She was not surprised that they were testing to see if her son was an incarnate lama. Two of her other sons had been recognized as such.

The Rinpoche's tests were tricky. He wanted to know if Lhamo could pick out things that belonged to the Thirteenth Dalai Lama (in other words, to see if the boy recognized his own belongings from his previous life). The Rinpoche took out two strands of black beads and asked Lhamo to choose the one that he liked the most. Without hesitating, Lhamo picked the beads that had belonged to the Thirteenth Dalai Lama and put them around his neck. The Rinpoche showed him two more strands of yellow beads and asked him to do the same.

Again Lhamo knew the right beads. The Rinpoche did the same thing with walking sticks and ivory drums. Lhamo never failed to recognize the right items.

The Rinpoche and his men all looked at each other in relief and deep happiness. Still, they could not give away the secret of who they had found. They didn't even tell Lhamo Dhondup's family.

AH, KA, MA

ཨ ཀ མ

SIX
Becoming a Monk Again

THE RINPOCHE AND HIS OFFICIALS TOLD Lhamo's family that the boy should be taken to Kumbum Monastery. Lhamo's parents were both pleased and saddened about leaving their three-year-old son at the monastery. They knew that it was an honor, but they were pained to lose their boy. Lhamo wailed when his mother left him. His father and older brother told him that his mother had gone to fetch watermelon. For days, Lhamo asked when she would return with the fruit.

Kumbum Monastery, Amdo, Tibet

Two of Lhamo's older brothers had already been brought to the monastery for their education. They were always busy with lessons and had little time to play with their younger brother. Lhamo liked to wait outside the door of the study room when Lobsang Samten was reciting his lessons. He peeked in at his brother and asked when he could come out to play. As soon as Lobsang was free, the two ran through the halls and explored the monastery chambers.

Young monks studying, Bodhnath, Nepal

Their stern-faced uncle, who was also a monk, became Lobsang Samten's guardian. Once, Lhamo crawled
over his uncle's scriptures and mixed up the loose pages.
For that, his uncle spanked him on the back side, and
Lhamo avoided him from then on.

Early one morning at the monastery, Lhamo was put
on a high throne. The Rinpoche and his officials sat in
front of him, looking serious and dignified. Lhamo gave
them blessings with his small hands, though nobody had
told him what to do.

Everyone believed that this was a sign that Lhamo
was indeed the reincarnation of the Thirteenth Dalai
Lama.

Yak, Central Tibet

SEVEN
Journey to the Lion Throne

SO THE FOURTEENTH DALAI LAMA HAD BEEN discovered. Now, the officials had to get him to Lhasa. This was not easy. First, there was the problem of transportation. The trip would take three months travelling on foot and on mule, since in those days there were no modern roads and very few automobiles in Tibet.

Second, at that time, part of eastern Tibet had been invaded by the Chinese and was under their control. The Chinese governor, Ma Bu Feng, was a greedy and dishonest man. As soon as he learned that the Dalai Lama was discovered in his district, he laid plans to profit from the situation.

At first Ma Bu Feng insisted that the child be accompanied to Lhasa by a large troop of Chinese soldiers. The Tibetans did not agree to this. They knew that the Chinese soldiers would remain in Lhasa after they had escorted the Dalai Lama to his palace. On top of that, the governor wanted money —lots of money— about the equivalent of 30,000 American dollars. This was a huge amount for Tibetans. But that was not all.

Potala Palace, Lhasa, Tibet

Just as soon as they paid this sum, Ma Bu Feng turned another trick. He demanded even more money, three times as much as the first amount. He made up excuses that more money was needed for the military protection of the Dalai Lama and for general government expenses.

The Tibetans had trouble coming up with this amount. After months of negotiating and planning, they found help. A group of Moslem merchants came to trade in the area. The Tibetans borrowed the money from the Moslems and promised to repay them in Lhasa. In one way, this was very lucky. The Dalai Lama could travel side by side with these Moslem traders who could protect the caravan against the robbers who roamed the wide Tibetan territories. And Ma Bu Feng agreed to let them go with an escort of only twenty Chinese soldiers.

Finally, the day came for departure. It was the first day of the sixth month of the Earth Hare year. Astrologers said that this was a lucky day for travelling. The four-year-old Dalai Lama travelled with his brother Lobsang Samten in a treljam. This is a decorated chair carried by two mules. Lhamo's mother, now named the Great Mother, also travelled in a treljam. The rest of the group walked or rode on horses or mules.

The Dalai Lama and his brother soon grew restless travelling this way. Sometimes they cried, and other times they argued. When they got too noisy, adults rode up beside the treljam and handed dried fruit to the boys— anything to keep them from fighting.

Every day for three months the group trekked from dawn until noon. Then they stopped to make camp and cook a meal. For days and days they saw no other human beings. They were lucky to avoid the thieves, wild animals and swarms of bees famous in Tibet.

From time to time near the end of the trip, people came to meet the young leader. They carried white scarves called katas which they offered in respect. A welcoming committee greeted the new Dalai Lama as he approached Lhasa. Hundreds of Tibetans and foreign government officials lined up to usher him to the Potala, the palace of the Dalai Lamas. People stood with their hands folded in front of their chests and smiled at the sight of their beloved leader. Some people even cried.

Soon after moving to Lhasa, the boy was placed on the great "Lion Throne of Tibet." Upheld by eight great snow lions carved and painted at its four corners, the Lion Throne is the traditional seat of the Dalai Lamas in Lhasa. In Tibet the snow lion, a mythical white lion with a green mane, symbolizes the fearless proclamation of the Buddhist religion.

The Dalai Lama always looked calm and patient during these ceremonies. At only four-and-a-half years old, this boy was already the spiritual leader of the Tibetans.

༄༅། །ཡར་རྒྱན་གྱི་གཤིས་ཀ་འབྲུག་ལོ། རྒྱལ་བརྒྱན་ཡོངས་རྫོགས་ཀྱི་པ་དགོས་འབྱུང་མེ་རྟོ་རྗེ་འཁར་དུ་འབྱེ་ནུ་རྣམས་རྒྱལ་ཡོ་བརྒྱ་བཞིའི་པ་ཆེ་ནཔ༌

The Dalai Lama, age ten

EIGHT
Eyes of the Telescope

THE YOUNG DALAI LAMA SPENT HIS LIFE IN Lhasa living in two palaces. The winter palace, the Potala, was built 400 feet above the city of Lhasa. It was almost one-quarter of a mile long and thirteen stories tall, one of the largest buildings in the world when it was built by the Fifth Dalai Lama in 1645. Constructed without cement or nails, the Potala was built from huge blocks of stone stacked one atop the other. The Potala has more than 1000 rooms, many spiral staircases, 10,000 altars, hundreds of religious paintings and more than 10,000 butterlamps. The building is also a burial place for the past Dalai Lamas who have been placed in tombs decorated in gold and gems.

Yaks in front of the Potala

To the young Dalai Lama, the Potala Palace seemed like a dark and scary place to live. He was afraid of the dark and often felt the deep burning sensation of fear. There were many rooms in the Potala, including his own bedroom, that were black from the smoke of butterlamps and the dust of centuries. His room had long, heavy curtains that stretched from the high ceiling to the floor, behind which ran families of rats. He was never afraid of the rats, however.

The Dalai Lama loved to explore the Potala with Lobsang Samten, who was the only other member of his family living in the palace. One of their favorite games was to run down dark hallways and make their guardians find them. The high officials were not pleased with these games. The monk guards were often scolded for playing along. They were supposed to keep the boys safe and away from the lowest rooms of the palace, which were dungeons for criminals.

In his free time, the Dalai Lama played with mechanical toys. He loved to take them apart and rebuild them. Friends and diplomats often sent him toy cars, boats and airplanes which he immediately dismantled. Once, he even took apart his watch to see how it worked. When he put it together again, he was pleased to find that it still ran.

The young Dalai Lama liked to climb up to the rooftop of the Potala and watch people in the city below through a telescope. This was his only informal contact with people who lived outside the palace. His own family lived in a house below the Potala and saw him once a month. Occasionally the Great Mother baked some pastries and carried them to her son as a treat. The Dalai Lama's own cook served only simple food, never the specialities that the Great Mother could make.

Not all the sights from his rooftop made him happy. On some days, herders would pass below the Potala as they took their yaks and sheep to the slaughter houses. The Dalai Lama couldn't stand to think of these animals being killed, and he arranged to save more than ten thousand of them.

NINE
To the Summer Palace

SPRING BROUGHT LIGHT-HEARTEDNESS TO the young leader. He moved to the summer palace called Norbulingka, which means Jewel Park. The palace walls enclosed a large garden of fruit and nut trees, vegetables and flowers. There was also a lake where he could feed the fish that came to the surface. Inside, the rooms were brighter than those in the Potala. This gave a lighter feeling to all of life there. Norbulingka felt much more like a warm home.

One thing made the Dalai Lama very happy at Norbulingka. There was a motor generator for electricity. It was always breaking down, and when he was older he had fun fixing it. He learned about mechanics and engineering this way.

He also loved to watch movies. An old Chinese monk knew how to show the movies given to the previous Dalai Lama. Among these films was one about King George of England. The Dalai Lama received a movie camera from a Tibetan delegation that went to the United States and a matching projector from a British delegation to Lhasa. With the help of an Austrian man, Heinrich Harrer, who was living in Lhasa, he had a special movie house built at Norbulingka. They built the power house apart from the cinema so the noise wouldn't bother the old lamas, who did not like the idea of all this modern entertainment.

Norbulingka, the summer palace, Lhasa, Tibet

The Dalai Lama asked his friend Heinrich Harrer to make a film of life in Lhasa. Harrer was one of the few Westerners who had ventured to Lhasa. He became a friend to many Tibetans, and a tutor to the Dalai Lama. Because of his personal contacts and his technical knowledge of the camera, he was the perfect person to film life in the capital city. He and the Dalai Lama showed this film in the movie house. When the old lamas saw themselves on screen, they burst into laughter. Later, the Dalai Lama himself made a film without instruction from anyone. Curiosity and cleverness taught him well.

TEN
Letters on the Board

THE DALAI LAMA DIDN'T HAVE MUCH TIME for people-watching and games. Ever since he was six years old he had to study hard. First he learned to read and write. His teacher made him write on a wooden board until his letters were correct. After eight months, he was given paper. He was tutored in reading and writing in the morning, and then he practiced recitation of lessons in the evening.

Like all young monks, the Dalai Lama had to memorize many lessons and prayers. Sometimes he was bored and tired of studying and he would cry. At first, the monks pampered him when he was tired, but he would continue to cry. Then the teachers decided to ignore his crying and look stern when he whined. If nobody paid attention, he stopped crying.

When he was twelve years old, he began the difficult religious study of Tibetan Buddhism. He learned that all beings depend on one another and that people have a responsibility to help each other. His teachers explained that everyone is reborn after death. If people are evil or greedy in one life, then they may have a dark and difficult next life. If they are good, loving and generous, they have a chance of returning to a life with many joys. Good actions produce happiness and bad actions produce suffering both for oneself and for others. This idea is called Karma.

One way the Dalai Lama learned about the nature of the mind was through meditation. He learned to make his mind very still and to concentrate on one thing. Sometimes he focused his attention on one object, and sometimes he concentrated on feelings of love and compassion. In this way he practiced meditation, and soon he became an expert.

Over the years, the Dalai Lama learned hundreds of religious books by heart, memorizing and reciting lines every day. The more he practiced, the better he understood the ideas. The boy became more curious and asked his teachers for advanced lessons. This study prepared him for philosophical debate.

The Dalai Lama's tutors, Ling Rinpoche (left) and Trijang Rinpoche (right)

Tibetan Buddhist students practice their lessons by asking each other difficult questions about the nature of the world and of the mind. This is called debate, and it is a good way to learn how to think quickly and clearly. The Dalai Lama was sharp in debate because he knew and understood the scriptures so well. As he grew up he became a respected student of Buddhism. Like other students he had to take many tests. He had to answer questions in front of many teachers and other pupils. His teachers asked him tricky questions, but the Dalai Lama always amazed them by his clear and thoughtful answers.

When he was twenty-four years old, the Dalai Lama was ready to take his final examinations. He was tested along with other monk-scholars during the great religious celebration that took place every year in Lhasa. For this day of testing, thousands of monks gathered at the Jokhang, Lhasa's most sacred temple, to listen to the Dalai Lama's careful answers. The test was difficult. The Dalai Lama had to answer questions with speed and precision, but nonetheless, he passed. He received the degree of Master of Metaphysics. The Dalai Lama knew then, however, that even though he had received his degree, he would never cease to learn.

Monks debating. The monk on the right claps his hands as he finishes asking his question.

ELEVEN
Invitation to Danger

A T THE SAME TIME THAT THE DALAI LAMA
was in religious training, his country was in tur-
moil. The Chinese had moved slowly into Lhasa
and were trying to take over the city little by
little. There was danger in the air and people could feel
it. Tibetans decided that they needed the Dalai Lama to
lead the government, even though he was only fifteen
years old. He had learned very little about government
and foreign affairs, but he was asked to take full control
of his country.

On the first of March in 1959, when the twenty-four-
year-old Dalai Lama was preparing to take his final
examinations in the Jokhang Temple, he received an invitation from the Chinese General Tan Kuan-sen sent
through two junior Chinese officers. They invited him to
watch a Chinese performance in their camp, and asked
for a date when he would be free. The Dalai Lama told
them that he would respond after he had taken his
exams. The officers were stubborn, and wanted a yes or
no right away. They asked again, but the Dalai Lama's
answer was the same. On the seventh of March, the
Dalai Lama was back at Norbulingka when he received
another message from the Chinese General. This time
the General's secretary asked about the performance
date, and the Dalai Lama set the time for the tenth of
March.

The Dalai Lama at age fourteen, seated on the Lion Throne and surrounded by his bodyguards

On the ninth of March, two Chinese officers came at 6:00 A.M. to Norbulingka. They asked Kusung Depon, the Commander of the Bodyguard, to return with them to the Chinese headquarters in order to prepare for the Dalai Lama's visit. Kusung Depon had not yet eaten breakfast, and told the Chinese men that he would come after eating and bathing. The officers left in a grumble, but soon returned with demands that Kusung Depon go with them immediately. The impatience of the Chinese stirred up suspicions.

At the headquarters, the General huffed with frustration, and spoke harshly to Kusung Depon.

"The Dalai Lama is coming here tomorrow. There are details to settle. That is why I sent for you. Don't you know that he has agreed to come tomorrow?" he bellowed.

"I was not aware that the date was set," answered Kusung Depon.

The General then demanded that the Dalai Lama come without his usual bodyguards, and insisted that his Tibetan attendants not carry weapons. This was an unusual request, one the Tibetan people would never approve. Kusung Depon was very careful when he asked the General why bodyguards were not allowed.

"We don't want trouble! And, this whole thing must be held secret," ordered the General.

Kusung Depon returned to Norbulingka to discuss the situation with the other Tibetan officials. All of the Dalai Lama's attendants were anxious that night. They could not rest. Even the Dalai Lama slept poorly because of worry. He rose at 5:00 AM to offer prayers, to meditate, and to watch the bright sun rise over the palace. Suddenly, a noise burst outside of the palace walls, and the Dalai Lama rushed inside to learn what had happened.

The townspeople had heard about the Chinese invitation and marched to the palace to surround it and protect their leader. They were angry and shouted out against the Chinese. The Dalai Lama was supposed to go to the Chinese headquarters at noon, but he couldn't pass through the crowd of his supporters.

The people cried, "The Chinese must go. Tibet for the Tibetans!"

Finally, the Dalai Lama asked his attendants to inform the Chinese General of the situation. At about noon, a Tibetan official shouted through a loudspeaker to tell the crowds that the visit was cancelled.

The people cheered, but would not go home.

When the Chinese General heard that the event was cancelled, he was furious. He burst with anger.

"Tibetan reactionaries! Now, we'll take drastic measures," he shouted.

The Dalai Lama (left) disguised as a foot soldier, during his escape from Tibet in 1959

TWELVE
Escape from Norbulingka

THE DALAI LAMA WANTED TO AVOID violence, but his people grew noisier and more determined to protect their leader and their city. On the sixteenth of March, rumors were spread that the Chinese were preparing for an attack. The Tibetans were ready to defend their leader, but they were no match for the Chinese guns and bombs. The Dalai Lama and his Cabinet decided that they must leave the palace in order to save the Tibetan people. They hoped that the Chinese would not fire if they couldn't find the Tibetan leader.

So, on the seventeenth of March, 1959, the Dalai Lama went to his temple. He prayed to the protector Mahakala and asked for strength to save his people, and for protection for all. Then he disguised himself as a common foot soldier. One devoted attendant stepped forward and offered his own rifle for the disguise.

The Tibetan officials had a scheme. Three escape parties left the palace at different times. The Dalai Lama went first, followed by the rest of his family and attendants who travelled on foot or on mule. They moved swiftly and silently to bypass Chinese soldiers, and then crossed the Tsang Po river in yak skin boats.

A patch of dark grey clouds cast a shadow over the escape party as it raced ahead in the dark. Tibetans across the plateau heard about the escape and came to secure their leader. One man named Tashi Norbu gave his prize white horse to the Dalai Lama—a perfect gift to replace the tired mules. The Dalai Lama saw this gift as a sign of good fortune.

One soldier rode from the capital and caught up with the escape party to report that the Chinese had bombed the summer palace. After the explosions, Chinese soldiers had rushed in to search for the dead body of the Dalai Lama. During three terrible days of fighting, more than 10,000 Tibetans were killed.

With this news, the escape party had no choice but to cross the border into India. The Dalai Lama's heart fell in sadness. He had wanted to save his people from a massacre and had hoped for a peaceful resolution. As he crossed the border, he thought about his brave countrymen. In India, he planned to find help for his country.

Crossing a mountain pass, Central Tibet

The Dalai Lama, 1989

T H I R T E E N
Teaching Compassion—
Working for Peace

THE DALAI LAMA HAS NEVER RETURNED to Tibet since he escaped in 1959. He now lives and works in Dharamsala, a small mountain village in India. He has set up a Tibetan democratic government-in-exile and a refuge for his people. Many Tibetans have fled their country in order to be free of Chinese control. Their leader helps them to build a happy life in exile while they all hope to return to a land of peace where they can practice their true way of life.

Even though he has seen so much suffering the Dalai Lama says that he is generally a happy man. One of his greatest wishes is to bring harmony between all people, and toward this end, he meets with leaders of other countries and with religious leaders. He travels throughout the world to talk about freedom, compassion, responsibility, environmental protection, friendship and inner happiness. He has been invited to speak in cathedrals, at universities, at world prayer centers, in government offices, on radio and on television.

Despite all of the tragedies he has seen, the Dalai Lama has never changed his mind about the importance of using peaceful means to establish peace between people and nations. He knows that violence only brings more violence, and he always says, "If you can't help people, at least don't hurt them." As people throughout the world have come to know this kind leader, they have understood his wisdom. They have understood that his work for peace deserves international recognition. And so, in 1989, people around the world rejoiced when the Dalai Lama was awarded the Nobel Prize for Peace.

The Dalai Lama is a man who can explain the most complicated matters in simple words, a man who strives to understand his neighbor in order to establish harmony. And above all, he is a man who laughs — whose gentle good humor and wide smile give away his kind heart.

The Dalai Lama receiving the Nobel Peace Prize from Mr. Egil Aarvik,
Chairman of the Norwegian Nobel Committee

Arriving in
India, 1959

In ceremonial dress,
Tibet, about 1950

Formal portrait, Tibet,
about 1954

Lecturing at
Middlebury College,
Vermont, 1984

Meeting with
aders, 1956

Greeting well-wishers, 1989

The Dalai Lama with members of his family. From left, the Great Mother, Tsering Dolma, Thubten Jigme Norbu, Gyalo Thondup, Lobsang Samten, the Dalai Lama, Jetsun Pema, and Tendzin Choegyal.

Family Tree

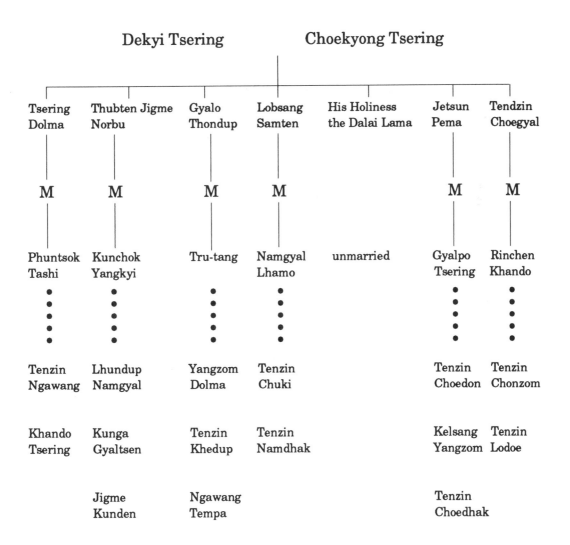

Dekyi Tsering   Choekyong Tsering

Tsering Dolma	Thubten Jigme Norbu	Gyalo Thondup	Lobsang Samten	His Holiness the Dalai Lama	Jetsun Pema	Tendzin Choegyal
M	M	M	M		M	M
Phuntsok Tashi	Kunchok Yangkyi	Tru-tang	Namgyal Lhamo	unmarried	Gyalpo Tsering	Rinchen Khando
Tenzin Ngawang	Lhundup Namgyal	Yangzom Dolma	Tenzin Chuki		Tenzin Choedon	Tenzin Chonzom
Khando Tsering	Kunga Gyaltsen	Tenzin Khedup	Tenzin Namdhak		Kelsang Yangzom	Tenzin Lodoe
	Jigme Kunden	Ngawang Tempa			Tenzin Choedhak	

M = Married

● ● ● ● ● = children

Word List

Buddhism   a religion spread by Siddhartha Gautama, who lived in India during the fifth century BCE

Butterlamp   a decorative cup or vessel that holds melted butter and a wick, which burns like a candle when lit

Compassion   the wish to free others from their suffering

Dalai Lama   an honorary title meaning "Ocean of Wisdom." The Dalai Lama is the spiritual and political leader of Tibet. The present Dalai Lama is the fourteenth.

Deity   embodiment of perfection

Exile   the state of being forced out of one's home land

Incarnate   a spirit reborn in a new body

Karma   the theory that all actions and thoughts produce effects in the future and thereby determine our future circumstances

Kata   a white ceremonial scarf offered in respect

Lama   a Tibetan Buddhist teacher

Mahakala   the buddha of compassion appearing as a fierce protector, the special protector of the Dalai Lamas

Meditation   a practice of deep concentration of the mind

Metaphysics   philosophy of the mind, of knowing

Monastery   a place where monks live together and practice their religion

Monk or nun   someone who devotes his or her life to a particular practice of religion

Offering   gifts offered to show respect

Regent   an appointed leader who governs while the Dalai Lama is a child or is absent

Rinpoche   the title for an incarnate lama, meaning "Precious One" in Tibetan

Scriptures   sacred religious books

Temple   building dedicated for religious worship

Tukpa   Tibetan noodle soup

Further Reading
for adults

Avedon, John. *In Exile from the Land of the Snows*. London: Michael Joesph, 1984.

Chophel, Norbu. *Folk Culture of Tibet*. Dharamsala: Library of Tibetan Works and Archives, 1983.

Dalai Lama, His Holiness the. *My Land and My People*. New York: McGraw Hill, 1962.

Goodman, Michael Harris. *The Last Dalai Lama*. Boston: Shambala, 1986.

Harrer, Heinrich. *Seven Years in Tibet*. New York: E. P. Dutton, 1954.

Hicks, Roger & Ngakpa Chogyam. *Great Ocean*. London: Element Books, 1984.

Norbu, Thubten J. & Heinrich Harrer. *Tibet is My Country*. London: Wisdom Publications, 1986.

Piburn, Sidney. *The Dalai Lama: A Policy of Kindness*. Ithaca, N.Y.: Snow Lion Publications, 1990.

Tung, Rosemary Jones. *A Portrait of Lost Tibet*. Ithaca, N.Y.: Snow Lion Publications, 1987.

Further Reading
for children

Gerstein, Mordicai. *The Mountains of Tibet*. New York: Harper & Row, 1987.

Ghose, Sudhin. *Tibetan Folk Tales and Fairy Stories*. Calcutta: Rupa & Co., 1986.

Gibb, Christopher. *The Dalai Lama*. (People who have helped the world). Milwaukee: Gareth Stevens Children's Books, 1990.

Gibb, Christopher. *The Land of Snows*. History of Tibet. Book 1. Dharamsala: Tibetan Children's Village, 1984.

Gibb, Christopher. *Independence to Exile*. History of Tibet. Book 2. Dharamsala: Tibetan Children's Village, 1987.

O'Conner, W. F. *Folk Tales from Tibet*. Kathmandu: Ratna Pustak Bhandar, 1977.

View from the roof of the Jokhang Temple, with the Dalai Lama's chambers in the foreground, Lhasa, Tibet

Photo Credits

Page 6. The Western Gateway to Lhasa, Tibet.
Photo: C. Sudyam Cutting.
Photograph courtesy of the Newark Museum.

12. The Dalai Lama at age four.
Photo courtesy of the Tibetan Information Office, Dharamsala.

14. Avalokiteshvara, the deity who represents perfect compassion.
Thangka, ca. 1975.
Courtesy of Sidney Piburn.

19. The Thirteenth Dalai Lama, ca. 1910-12
Photo: T. H. Paar.
Photograph courtesy of the Newark Museum.

23. Ah, Ka, Ma
Calligraphy by Pema Losang Chogyen.

24. Kumbum Monastery, Amdo, Tibet; ca. 1985.
Photo: Zasep Tulku.

25. Young monks studying, Bodhnath, Nepal, ca. 1977.
Photo: Sidney Piburn.

26. Yak, Central Tibet.
Photo: Steven Squyres.

28. Potala Palace, Lhasa, Tibet.
Photo: C. Sudyam Cutting.
Photograph courtesy of the Newark Museum.

31. The Dalai Lama, age ten.
Photographer unknown.
Collection of the Newark Museum. Cutting gift 1982.

32. Yaks in front of the Potala Palace, Lhasa.
Photo: C. Sudyam Cutting.
Photograph courtesy of the Newark Museum.

35. Norbulingka, the summer palace, Lhasa.
Photo: C. Sudyam Cutting.
Photograph courtesy of the Newark Museum.

37. The Dalai Lama's tutors, Ling Rinpoche (left) and Trijang Rinpoche (right), India,
ca. 1975. Photograph courtesy of the Tibetan Information Office, Dharamsala.

39. Monks debating, Tashilunpo Monastery, Shigatse, Tibet, 1986.
Photo: Peter Gold.

41. The Dalai Lama at age fourteen, Lhasa.
    Photo © Lowell Thomas, Jr. 1990.
    Photograph courtesy of Marist College.

44. The Dalai Lama (left) disguised as a foot soldier during his escape from Tibet in
    1959. Photo courtesy of the Tibetan Information Office, Dharamsala.

47. Crossing a mountain pass, Central Tibet.
    Photo: C. Sudyam Cutting.
    Photograph courtesy of the Newark Museum.

48. The Dalai Lama, 1989. Photo: Don Farber/Thubten Dhargye Ling.

51. Receiving the Nobel Peace Prize from Mr. Egil Aarvik, Chairman of the
    Norwegian Nobel Committee. Photo: Rajiv Mehrotra.

54. With members of his family, ca. 1960.
    Photo courtesy of the Tibetan Information Office, Dharamsala.

59. View from the roof of the Jokhang Temple, Lhasa, Tibet, ca. 1986.
    Photo: Peter Gold.

Photo spread, pages 52-53

In ceremonial dress, Tibet, ca. 1950. Photo courtesy of the Tibetan Information
Office, Dharamsala.

Formal portrait, Tibet, ca. 1954.
Photo courtesy of the Tibetan Information Office, Dharamsala.

Arriving in India, 1959.
Photo courtesy of the Tibetan Information Office, Dharamsala.

Meeting with leaders in India, 1956. Left to right: Zhao Enlai, Pandit Nehru, the
Dalai Lama, the Panchen Lama. Photo courtesy of the Tibetan Information
Office, Dharamsala.

Lecturing at Middlebury College, Vermont, 1984.
Photographer unknown.
Courtesy of the Office of Tibet, New York.

Greeting well-wishers following the Nobel award, 1989. Photo: Rajiv Mehrotra.

Map

Reprinted by permission of the Newark Museum.
Drawing by Bruce Pritchard.

Tibetan Children's Village

The Tibetan Children's Village was established in Dharmasala, India, in 1960 by His Holiness the Dalai Lama. His vision was that the caring and education of Tibetan children should be placed foremost in the affairs of the Tibetan refugee community. Now directed by Mrs. Pema Gyalpo, His Holiness' sister, the Village is the primary caring center for orphaned and destitute Tibetan children in India.

Relying solely on donations from individuals and relief agencies, the Village strives to provide adequate food, housing and education to these young Tibetans. The work is hampered by a tremendous overcrowding problem and a continual influx of children coming from Chinese occupied Tibet.

Many of these children are in need of sponsor families. Those sponsors who want to offer both funds and friendship to their sponsored child may obtain more information by contacting the author through Snow Lion Publications, P.O. Box 6483, Ithaca, NY 14851.